THE CALL

Guide for Leaders
and Facilitators

Francois Carr

The CALL—Guide for Leaders and Facilitators

Editor: Wilna Swart
Book design and layout: Lizelle Steenkamp

First published in 2021 by The Connected Life Ministries.

CONTENTS

And He went up on the mountain and called to Him those He Himself wanted. And they came to Him. Then He appointed twelve; **that they might be with Him** *and that He might send them out to preach, and to have power to heal sicknesses and to cast out demons.*
Mark 3:13–15 (See also Matthew 10:1–4, Luke 6:12–16)

And He called the twelve to Himself, and **began to send them out** *two by two, and gave them power over unclean spirits. He commanded them to take nothing for the journey except a staff—no bag, no bread, no copper in their money belts—but to wear sandals, and not to put on two tunics.* **So, they went out** *and preached that people should repent. And they cast out many demons, and anointed with oil many who were sick, and healed them.*
Mark 6:7–9, 12–14 (See also Matthew 10:5–20, Luke 9:1–6, Luke 10:1–24)

Then the apostles **gathered to Jesus** *and told Him all things, both what they had done and what they had taught. And He said to them,* **"Come aside** *by yourselves to a deserted place* **and rest a while.**"
Mark 6:30–31

Introduction to the Study Guide

Welcome to *The Call—Guide for Leaders and Facilitators.*

I am pleased that God has led you to become part of this 'discipleship process.' It is as much a personal journey for you as it is for the person or group that you disciple, mentor or coach.[1] Something I have learned in order to keep growing in my own spiritual life is that I need to read good books and have like-minded friends. In addition, it is also wise to cultivate a mentoring relationship with your own mentor or coach, who can keep you accountable. Second, spend some time with a good friend or trusted person who can encourage and challenge you. Third, I want to encourage you to read good supplementary material. Last, share continuously with others what you are learning by investing your time and your life in the lives of others (2 Timothy 2: 1–2).

LeRoy Eims, in his book *The Lost Art of Disciple Making*, explains that every believer in Jesus Christ deserves an opportunity to be nurtured personally and with a view to their development. But all too often the opportunity is lacking. We neglect the young Christian in our whirl of programs, church services, and fellowship groups. And we fail to raise up workers and leaders who can disciple young believers to become mature and fruitful Christians. Eims says, 'True growth takes time and tears and love and patience.'[2] Jesus came to save the world, and to that end He died, but on His way to the cross He concentrated His life on making 12 disciples. These men were in turn taught to make disciples until, through the process of reproduction, the gospel of the kingdom reaches the ends of the earth.[3]

What will happen if we follow the example of Jesus by taking the time to connect, share, develop, and invest our time and lives in those whom Jesus has brought into our lives at this very moment (See John 13:20)? The words *potential* and *opportunity* come to mind. Just imagine this: everyone in your group has reached his or her full potential by living and acting like Jesus and duplicating and multiplying themselves in others.

End Product of a Disciple

We are all called to be disciples, sent out to be witnesses and represent Him in every aspect of our lives (*The Call*, 135–137). However, it is important to keep the end product of a disciple in mind as we mentor and seek to help people. When God looks at people, He only sees their heart and potential, what they are meant to be and become, and not what they are at present. You must look at the people whom God has uniquely brought into your life with the same perspective.

What is the end product? It is to:

- Pursue Christlikeness;
- Become a solid, dedicated, committed, fruitful and spiritually mature believer;
- Become an effective laborer in the harvest who, in time, can disciple someone else.

Cycle of Discipleship

It is clear in the Scriptures that Jesus took ordinary men, converts, whose names have been entered in the book of life (See Luke 10:20), trained and developed them into workers and leaders. Remember, the process of transformation and the cycle of discipleship that Jesus followed with His disciples comprise three main parts:

1. Being with Jesus
2. Being changed and transformed by Jesus
3. Being sent for Jesus

The Goals and Objectives of The Call and The Call—Study Guide

I would like to emphasize the importance of the goals and objectives of *The Call* and *Study Guide*. Once you've studied all the material, and completed the questions and assignments, you will look back and realize you have pursued and hopefully reached some of the goals and objectives of *Connecting your Life with God's Call and Purpose*. It is important to keep in mind, as you mentor someone or a group, that:

- we realize God has a plan and a purpose for you;
- we must be connected with God and stay connected;
- we enjoy a personal devotional life and keep a journal;
- we are able to write our own stories of salvation;
- we become aware of our circles of influence and share our stories of salvation;
- we learn how to be relational and intentional, to listen, and to ask questions.

In closing, create a simple written plan of your intentions. Keep the focus on the goals, objectives, questions and assignments of each chapter and session. Be sensitive to the needs of your group of mentees and how the Lord deals with them. Finally, regardless of how you decide to use this resource:

Enjoy the journey!

---

1. Paul D. Stanley and J. Robert Clinton, in their book *Connecting—The Mentoring Relationships You Need to Succeed in Life*, explain that mentoring is a relational experience in which one person empowers another by sharing God-given resources. They say that there are different kinds of relationships with the potential to empower a person who desires to learn and grow. This includes being a Discipler, Spiritual Guide, Coach, Counselor, Teacher and Sponsor (NavPress in alliance with Tyndale Publishers, 1992, 33). In this guide we will use the word Mentor/Mentee and Connecting for the sake of consistency and clarity.
2. LeRoy Eims, *The Lost Art of Disciple Making* (Grand Rapids, Michigan: Zondervan, 1978), Blurb
3. Ibid., 9

Knowing about God is fascinating but knowing God personally is life-changing.

Guidelines for Leaders/Facilitators

The *Leader* or *Facilitator* of the study guide for *The Call* comes alongside participants so that they can help them to adopt a new lifestyle of intimacy with God, be transformed into the image of Jesus Christ, and join Him on His mission to reach and change the world. You have heard and responded to God's invitation to come alongside someone, lead a small group or facilitate an I Connect Cohort. I want to give you some thoughts and insights that will help you to prepare for your 'assignment' from God.

What Not to Do?

Much of the *Study Guide* and this *Guide for Leaders and Facilitators* is written from the understanding that you have attended the training, a retreat or worked through *The Call*-related material yourself. Each lesson will challenge you to look at your own personal leadership development, skills and experience as you prepare to spend time with those whom you will mentor (disciple).[4] Trust the process! It takes time to process truth, spiritual insights and growth: yours and that of those whom you lead. Be patient. Only move towards the next step when you feel ready to do so.

Remember, it is not what you know, but what you or your 'disciple' will become that is important.

Bible Study

The *Study Guide* is not a Bible study for individuals or for small groups, but is designed as a Discipleship tool that teaches you how to ask questions, to learn how to listen to others, invest time in the lives of others, share your insights, and be transparent before others. However, you can use *The Call* along with the *Connecting my Life— Questions and Discussions* in this guide to apply the same truths in a Bible study setting.

Spiritual Preparation

The *Study Guide*, which you will need, has already been prepared for you. You need a copy of the book *The Call*, a Bible, notebook and pen. If you are a *Leader* or *Facilitator* of a group, you also need the *Guide for Leaders and Facilitators*, which you are reading right now. Furthermore, it will be for your own benefit in your preparation if you:

- Spend time reading through the relevant chapters in *The Call* as and when they connect with your session. Then read through the relevant questions and the assignment in the *Study Guide*. Write down and meditate on the truth God reveals to your heart. Remember, first read everything for yourself and then do so to prepare yourself to get the most out of your one-on-one coaching or small-group session. The Process of Transformation and Cycle of Discipleship, as explained in *The Call*, will be changing and repeating itself constantly as you grow in understanding on your walk with God.
- *Trust the Holy Spirit* to be your teacher. Ask Him for guidance as you reflect on the truths, how they apply to your life and how they affect your walk, especially as you prepare for a discipling session. Release your mind and heart in ready obedience to everything He reveals to you and teaches you.
- *Pray* sincerely for yourself, and for your session. Pray in response to what the Holy Spirit shows or teaches you.
- Keep a *spiritual journal* of God's activity in your life. It is important to record all that God is saying to you, or a word or promise God gave you for your group. You may not always recall these special moments, but your journal will. Your

written record is also an indication of your own growth and character development.
- Make some *notes* under the relevant session in your *Study Guide* that might be helpful as you coach someone or a group.

Discipleship and Coaching

This is a 10- to 12-week/month process after the *First Meeting—Note from the Author* had commenced. However, this can be adjusted for a longer or shorter time frame, depending on the needs, limits and preferences of the individual or group you are discipling. Remember, the goal is not just to work through the questions or sessions but to connect with God, and with one another, which leads to the spiritual transformation that only comes from the Holy Spirit. You can meet once a week or every second week or once a month until the process has been completed. Be careful not to rush it.

One-on-One

The best environment for discipleship is one-on-one and face-to-face time spent with one another. We communicate verbally by talking with one another, but non-verbal communication (body language, hand gestures, verbal intonation, eye contact, and other physical aspects) gives new and unspoken insight and information. Sometimes the non-verbal communication will strengthen or shift the process to a different conversation or in another direction. Our dependence on and sensitivity to the Holy Spirit is our guide to success in this.

Meeting with another believer in a neutral environment, shaking hands, spending an hour together and praying will give a sense of intimacy and like-mindedness, establish unity and emphasize the importance of what God is doing. We are not just following His example by being relational and investing time, but also building a relationship of trust.

However, we recognize that busy schedules necessitate different venues for the various processes to take place. Most of the venues that are available will fit the purpose. You can also use the internet (Skype, Zoom), FaceTime or any other available media. It will not give you the same feeling as being there in person, but it is the next best thing. The telephone is also an acceptable method of coaching, but it is the least preferred method.

One-on-Some (Small Group)

Although individuals can be mentored, a small-group environment is also effective for studying these principles. Members can meet for weekly accountability sessions, have discussions, watch video segments of *The Call,* and conclude with the questions, and the truths that had been gained. Although the group has a Leader/Facilitator, this person will not lead the group as in a typical Bible study, but rather lead and serve through coordinating and facilitating the group session. The Leader can ask the questions relating to the relevant sessions, giving ample time for responses, so that each participant answers the question and not just a few in the group. Or the Leader can ask each member to participate by rotating the asking of questions, while allowing everyone in the group to answer every question and listen to the answers.

We suggest that small groups (one-on-some) do not exceed a total of four members. More members per group may reduce the level of intimacy, transparency, growth and maturity as well as long-term effectiveness. It is also important to keep the time factor in mind as a session can become too long and time-consuming when everyone participates. Although Jesus had twelve disciples, He confided in three who were close to Him. If a pastor wants to disciple his elders and deacons or members, then it is advisable to have more than one group. However, the group can also be a one-on-many (I Connect Cohort or twelve people and more) but then the meeting time must be extended to give all the participants enough time to share.

Who will be discipled? A small group study is appropriate for people in home groups, Bible study groups, accountability groups, and prayer groups who participated in a retreat, or responded as a result of your Concentric Circles of Concern.

Where will we meet? You can meet at the church, in a home, for a meal at a local restaurant, or at a coffee shop; anywhere conducive to discussion and prayer.

When will we get together? Get together at a time that will be convenient for your group.

How long will we meet? Plan and aim for the session to last about an hour to allow for discussion and prayer. However, allow the Holy Spirit to determine and control the conversation and schedule.

What Must I Do?

Jesus said, '*The wind blows where it wishes, and you hear the sound of it, but cannot tell where it comes from and where it goes*' (John 3:8 NKJV). We cannot change or transform people's lives, but we can lay the foundation for the Holy Spirit to do so. Someone once said that we set the 'sails' to catch the wind, allowing the Holy Spirit to move. The *Study Guide* and the *Guide for Leaders and Facilitators* aim to help you 'set the sails' as we encounter and connect with God, and allow Him to transform our minds, hearts and lives as we walk through the coaching process. We need to keep in mind the objectives and focus points (see Appendix 1) of the guide and of every individual session as we prepare each session's coaching. We need to remember that the effectiveness of every session is determined by what happens *before*, *during* and *after* the discipleship and coaching processes.

Before

You have been assigned to mentor a person one-on-one or lead a small group. Are you wondering where to begin? Are you asking yourself these questions: Where do I start? What steps can I follow? What is expected of me? What do I do next? It is easy. You have already started. *The Call, The Call—Study Guide* and the resource in your hand can serve as your guide for the journey. The following are some simple guidelines you might want to consider, and perhaps follow:

- Contact the person or group and make an appointment.
- Set the date and time of your meeting and agree on the place where you will meet.
- Prepare yourself (see *Spiritual Preparation*).
- Read through the resources, the manual and questions set for the meeting.

- Write down some insights and any direction received from the Holy Spirit.
- For consecutive meetings, reflect on the previous meeting, its notes and assignments.
- Determine the objective of the next session.
- Decide what part of *The Call*, or which questions in the *Study Guide*, is important for this meeting.
- Leave for your appointment early and be at your meeting on time.
- If someone misses a session, get in touch with that person as soon as possible.

During

It is important to create an atmosphere of intimacy and trust to share and be able to talk about the goals and questions. Start the session by relating to one another and enquire what is happening in his/her life at that moment. Remember the person is more important than ticking off another coaching question or session.

At some point you need to redirect the conversation to what is happening in their spiritual life and walk with God.

It is very important not to do all the talking but to spend more time listening to what they are saying, and especially to the leading, prompting and guidance of the Holy Spirit. He will prompt you to ask the right questions. He is the ultimate coach, who knows and understands the needs of the person. Thus, listen with the intent to care and understand.

Remember that Jesus asked great questions and even answered questions with questions. Your questions should be thought-provoking and should lead to even deeper reflections, questions and insights. Remember, you do not need to cover or even touch on every question. It might be necessary to take notes as a reminder to return to certain topics or issues during the next session.

The following are some guidelines to keep in mind during discussions: See Appendix 2 for an example outline of a Group Meeting.

- Welcome and greet one another.
- Relate with one another—what's happening in your life?
- What's happening in your spiritual life and walk with God?
- Establish the objective of the appointment and keep that in mind.
- Ask some questions in the session notes.
- Listen and give your full attention to what each person is saying.
- Keep eye contact.
- Briefly summarize the conversations at some point.
- Give homework or set a goal to keep one another accountable.
- Confirm the goal and objective of the next appointment.
- Set the date and place of the next appointment.
- Pray and depart.

After

To disciple someone is to make a lasting investment in the life of another person and in the kingdom of God. Therefore, it is important to take a moment to reflect on your session and process the information by allowing the Holy Spirit to confirm or convict or change the direction of your meetings.

- Write down a summary of your discussion (one or two sentences should suffice).
- Write down the homework or assignment (as an accountability check).
- Highlight some commitments made or actions decided on.
- You can also email your summary to the mentee(s).
- Pray for the person(s).
- Send a text, email or make a phone call after and before the next meeting, staying in contact.
- Plan for and schedule your preparation in your calendar before the next meeting.

---

4. We encourage you to read all the books listed in the Recommended Reading section. Although many good books are available on the market, these will help you see and understand the objectives of training a disciple, worker and leader as well as establishing the relationships that will make a difference in your life.

God always gives enough strength for the next step.

First Meeting

The initial purpose of your *First Meeting* is to establish your 'discipling' relationship. Second, to talk about your mentee's or the small group's experiences and impressions of the recent retreat, training or reading of the *Note by the Author* in the book *The Call* and how this relates to their daily lives and God's purpose and agenda for them. Third, agree to meet once a week, every second week or once a month, or as long as it may take to continue the conversation or do the coaching. Last, determine and assign the roles of group members if you want to rotate the asking of questions.

Guidelines for your One-on-One Conversation

Step 1—Welcome and greet one another.

Step 2—Relate with the person. Ask the question: What is currently happening in your life, family or business? Listen carefully to the response, ask more questions and give attention to any emotions you pick up. Make a mental note (and write it down later) of what is said so that you can pray about or follow up on it. Remember not to rush through this part of the conversation as it is part of your objective—to build and establish a relationship of trust so that they would want to meet again. Pray for your mentee right there and then if necessary.

Step 3—Establish the main objective of the appointment. Share

1

with the person that this meeting is just to talk about their experiences and impressions of the recent retreat, school of prayer or reading of *The Call* and ask if they would like to meet again in the future to spend some time with you to summarize and recap the information they had received to help them make it their own.

Step 4—You can start the conversation by asking the questions. Listen carefully for any insights or remarks that you can respond to with another question or further insights.

You are welcome to read the section *God is Searching* in the *The Call* (pp. 130–132) or share your insights of that section. The purpose is not to teach or preach but simply to let the person know that God is looking for someone He can bless and that they could just be that person.

Here are some questions that you might want to consider asking as they are relevant, and you can use them in any setting. They will help you to focus on the goals, the reality of where you/they are at the moment, the possible options or actions that can be taken and may influence their willingness to begin.

- What was your experience or impression of the retreat/school of prayer/*The Call* material?
- What do you think God said in general or wants to say through *The Call*?
- What has God said to you personally? Any specific insights that you have gained?
- Are there any examples you need to follow?
- Are there any commands to obey?
- How will it affect your life/marriage/family/workplace if you apply this to your life?
- What freedom or liberty will you experience if you apply this to your life?
- Are there any changes you must make regarding your current lifestyle or routine?
- How do you think your life will be different if you make these changes in your life?
- What would you need to do now in responding to God?
- When will you start to apply these changes or goals?
- How can I help you to accomplish any of them?

2

You may feel you should ask questions such as the following instead:

- What do you sense God is saying to you?
- What adjustments do you need to make in your life?
- What is the next step you will take? When will you take that step?
- Who can help you to grow in this area?
- How can we pray for you about this step of faith?

Now either follow Steps 5 to 7, which are presented below, continue with your conversation or schedule another meeting before moving on through the steps. You do not have to complete every step or ask all the questions in one session. It is the beginning of the coaching relationship and it takes time to cultivate trust and to build the right foundation. Just remember, if your *First Meeting* turns into a *Second Meeting* you have already reached one of your objectives. Remember to revisit and reflect on the promises and commitments made during your First Meeting.

Step 5—Share your willingness to meet on a regular basis and talk about the steps and principles that are taught in *The Call*. If the person agrees, discuss some expectations and a timeline for these meetings and set the date and time of the next appointment.

Step 6—Briefly summarize the content of your discussion and include possible changes and action steps that need to be implemented.

Step 7—Pray together or for each other.

Follow-up after *First Meeting*

If your first meeting exceeds the time limit and turns into a second meeting, follow the same steps as with your first meeting. Although the overall objectives are the same, the objective of this *Second Meeting* is to reflect on the remainder of the questions suggested for the *First Meeting* as well as completing discussions and considering commitments made. The questions in Step 4 are more 'pointed,' namely:

- What has happened in your life (and/or spiritual life) since our meeting?
- What changes have you made since we met?

- How did that affect your life? Family? Marriage? Workplace?
- What are some of the reasons you did not apply any changes?
- What are some of the hindrances or obstacles that prevented you from starting?
- What can you do to change that and start applying it?
- How can I help?

Guidelines for your One-on-Some or One-on-Many (Small Group) Conversation

Step 1—Welcome and greet one another.

Step 2—Relate with the persons in the group. Share with one another what is currently happening in your lives, families and businesses or jobs. The purpose is to establish your relationship and encourage willingness in the group members to share with one another about their lives and being transparent about what is currently happening. Listen to what the members of the group are sharing and take the time, if needed, to pray for one another before continuing.

Step 3—Establish the objective of the appointment. Share with everyone that the objective of this meeting is to talk about their experiences and impressions of the recent retreat or school of prayer or reading of *The Call* to lay the foundation for a relationship of trust and to determine the roles of the group members. Although there is an initial leader, or facilitator, the goal is to develop and mature the group members to become growing disciples, workers and leaders by using the method and strategy of Jesus.

Step 4—The *Leader/Facilitator* assigns a role or number to each person for the session. Each person will be requested to ask a question according to their role and number. Everyone in the group should answer all the questions. The spinoff is that group members are taught how to invest time (being relational), ask questions, be transparent, speak in front of people, learn how to listen and observe as well as redirect questions. Once the arrangements for the asking of questions have been finalized, you can proceed with the conversation and let each person ask their question. The 4 Questions x 4 Answers per person therefore equals 16 responses that you may expect to receive.

The *Leader/Facilitator* must make a note of all the answers, insights and remarks to respond appropriately later.

Perhaps this is a good time to read *God is Searching* in *The Call* (pp. 130–132) or to share your insights of that section with the group members. The purpose is not to teach or preach but simply to let them know that God is looking for someone or people He can bless and it could be any or all of us.

The following is an example of a question set that you can follow or adjust according to your own preference.

Round 1:
- Person 1: What were your experiences or impressions of *The Call*?
- Person 2: What do you think God said in general or wants to say through *The Call*?
- Person 3: What did God say to you personally? Have you gained any insights?
- Person 4: How will that/they affect your life, marriage, family and workplace if you apply it/them in your life?

Round 2:
- Person 1: What liberty will you experience if you apply the change(s) in your life?
- Person 2: Are there any changes you must make to your current lifestyle?
- Person 3: What do you suppose your life would look like when you have made these changes?
- Person 4: Are there any examples to follow?

Round 3:
- Person 1: Are there any commands to follow?
- Person 2: What will you need to do in responding to God?
- Person 3: When will you start to work on that?
- Person 4: What would you need to do now in responding to God?

Leader:
- When will you start to apply these changes or goals?
- With whom can you share this coming week what you have learned or experienced?
- How can I help you to accomplish any changes or goals?

Follow Steps 5 to 7, which are presented below, continue your conversation, or you can schedule another meeting before moving on to the next session. You do not have to complete every step or ask all the questions in one session. It is the beginning of the coaching relationship and it takes time to cultivate trust and build the right foundation. After Round 1, you might sense that it would be best not to continue owing to restricted time or other constraints. You may decide instead to continue at a second meeting. This will give you some time to revisit and reflect on some of the promises and commitments made.

Step 5—If everybody agrees to meet for a second time to discuss some of the more pointed, direct questions in Round 2, ask about some expectations of and objectives for the planned meeting and set the date and time. Decide who will be Persons 1 to 4 so that they can prepare.

Step 6—Briefly summarize the content of your discussion and include possible changes and actions that need to be implemented.

Step 7—Pray together or for each other.

Follow-up after *First Meeting*

If your *First Meeting* turns into a *Second Meeting*, you can follow the same steps as with the *First Meeting*. Although the overall objectives are the same, the objective of this session is to reflect on the decisions that have been made and to discuss the questions in Round 2. The questions in Step 4 will be more 'pointed' or specific, as you will see when you read on.

Leader
- Welcome the group and open the session with prayer.
- What is happening in your life?
- What has been happening in your spiritual life since our last meeting?
- What changes have you made in your current lifestyle or routine because of what God revealed to you during our *First Meeting*, the reconnect retreat, school of prayer or since we last met?
- How did that affect your life? Family? Marriage? Workplace?
- What will you need to do in responding to God?

- When will you start to work on that?
- What are some of the reasons why you have not yet done so?
- What are some of the hindrances or obstacles that prevent you from starting?
- What can you do to change that and start applying the changes?
- How can I or we as a group help you to accomplish that?

In closing, remember the questions listed above are just a guideline to help you process information. Do not forget to look at and ask the questions in the *Study Guide*, while keeping in mind the goals, objectives, focus points, and assignments.

Appendix 1

Focus Points

All page references in Appendix 1 refer to The Call—Be and become the follower you are meant to be.

Note from the Author
Process of Transformation (*The Call*, xviii)
Cycle of Discipleship (xviii, xx)
Assignment: God has a purpose and plan for your life. Write down in a sentence what you think it is, and how your current life and activities match it.

The Call: Introduction
Being Shaped for a Purpose (5)
To Know Jesus and Be Known by Him (6–10)
To Follow His Method, Strategy and Example (10–13)
The Forgotten Jesus Model (13–15)
Assignment: Write a paragraph of how God has shaped, prepared and worked in your life until this moment.

Chapter 1: The Cause—*Continue With What Jesus Started*
Jesus' Favorite Mountain (17–21)
The Great Commission (22–25)
The Challenge (26–28)
Assignment: What comes to mind when you think about the Great Commission? How will this impact your life or schedule this coming week? Write down your thoughts and intentions.

Chapter 2: The Connection—*To Be With Him Before We Work For Him*
The Priorities (29–33)
Celebrity or Obedient Servant (34–35)
What Did Jesus Do? (35–39)

Appendix 2

Example Outline of Group Meeting[5]

Welcome the Group.
Open with Prayer (or ask someone to pray).

Looking Back

1. Care and Celebrate—Share any highlights/lowlights since you last met. Listen to the feedback and watch the body language and facial expressions of the people—respond to that by encouraging them, asking more questions, praying for someone or simply giving thanks to God.

2. Ask questions for accountability—Did you read through the assigned portion in the book? Did you watch the video clip? Did you complete the Survey questions and reflect on some of the contents of *Connecting My Life—Reflection and Discussion?* Did you work on your assignments? How did you obey the lesson from our last meeting? Did you pray with anyone in need? Did you share a Bible story, the Jesus story or your own story? With whom and what happened? Did you find a person or home of peace?[6] You may even want to add some of the default questions proposed for the First Meeting.

Looking Up

3. Refer to the assigned portion or chapter for the day. Highlight the focus point and content of the passage. Ask the group members to explain to you or tell you in their own words what they read, learned or remembered.

4. Use some of the *Connecting My Life—Reflection and Discussion* questions or the First Meeting questions.

Looking Forward

5. Talk about or practise a skill related to what you have learned.
6. Set goals for the next meeting and pray together. Ask these questions:

- What do you need to do this week to obey what you have learned?
- With whom could you share this passage, your story or the gospel story?

Confirm the date, time and place of the next meeting.
Close in Prayer.

---

5. Adapted from the *Discovery Bible Study*, Appendix 3.
6. Francois Carr, *The Call*, pp. 138–139.

Appendix 3

Discovery Bible Study and Three-Thirds Discipleship

Steve Addison, in his book *Pioneering Movements*, explain that the Discovery Bible Study is a simple and immediately transferable obedience-oriented method of making disciples. The method is profound because the Holy Spirit is present even when new disciples gather round the living Word of God to learn and obey. It is effective in discipling people to conversion, in foundational discipleship and in long-term discipleship. It is a core component of church-planting movements throughout the world. Here is one example of Discovery Bible Study within a Three-Thirds Discipleship framework. This outline can be adapted for meeting with seekers for foundational and long-term discipleship. It can also form the outline for a new church gathering. How have people obeyed what they learned last time? Has anyone shared the passage with someone?[7]

First Third: Look Back

1. Care
   - Share any highlights/lowlights since you last met.
   - Pray for one another.

2. Worship God together in a simple and relevant way.

3. Ask questions for accountability:
   - How did you obey the lesson in our last meeting?
   - Did you pray with anyone in need? Did you share a Bible story, a Jesus story or your own story? With whom and what happened? Did you find a person or home of peace?
   - *You can adapt this part to reflect on Review in The Call (Author).*

4. Casting Vision (*The Great Commission* and the *Concentric Circles of Concern*—Author).

- Take a few moments to 'cast vision' for lost people or making disciples.
- Pray for people who are lost or whom you have connected with who need God.

Second Third: Look Up

5. Read the new passage (Stories). Without looking at the text, retell the passage or story in your own words. Then ask:
   - What is the story or passage teaching or telling me about God or Jesus or Holy Spirit?
   - What does the story teach us about people?
   - Is there a command to obey or an example to follow?
6. *The Call*—here we deal with and study the passage relevant to the meeting and *Connecting My Life—Reflection and Discussion* (Author).

Final Third: Look Forward

7. Talk about or practise a skill related to what you have learned.
8. Set goals and pray together. Ask:
   - What do you need to do this week to obey what you have learned?
   - With whom could you share this passage, the gospel story or your story?

---

7. Addison, Steve, *Pioneering Movements, Leadership that Multiplies Leaders and Churches* (Downers Grove, Ill.: IVP, 2015), 171–173.

Appendix 4

Recommended Reading

David Watson and Paul D. Watson's, *Contagious Disciple Making: Leading Others on a Journey of Discovery* (Nashville, Tenn.: Thomas Nelson, 2014) will teach you more about the Discovery Bible Study.

Joel Rosenberg and T.E. Koshy, *The Invested Life: Making Disciples of All Nations One Person at a Time* (Carol Stream, Ill.: Tyndale House, 2012). Every follower of Jesus Christ should be able to answer two simple questions. Who is investing in me? Who am I investing in? God desires to pour an abundance of spiritual and emotional capital into your life—directly and through older and wiser believers. And He wants to use you to pour spiritual and emotional capital into the lives of others. Unfortunately, many Christians have never had someone disciple them or show them how to make a disciple. *The Invested Life* will teach you how to do that.

LeRoy Eims, *The Lost Art of Discipleship* (Grand Rapids, Mich.: Zondervan, 1978). LeRoy explains how the early church discipled new Christians; how to meet the basic needs of a growing Christian; how to identify any potential workers and how to develop mature, godly leaders. You will benefit from reading this book.

Paul D. Stanley and J. Robert Clinton, *Connecting—The Mentoring Relationships You Need to Succeed in Life* (Carol Stream, Ill.: NavPress in alliance with Tyndale House, 1992). We were meant for each other. The question is: How to find the right mentors, even when it seems none are available. By pointing to the seven different types of mentoring influences, the authors dispel the notion that there is only one 'ideal mentor' for each of us, and they show how it's possible never to be without at least one active mentoring relationship. They also discuss the three dynamics of successful mentoring and how mentoring can work for you right now, in whatever stage of life you find yourself.

Steve Smith with Ying Kai, T4T: *A Discipleship Re-Revolution* (Monument, Colo.: WIG Take Resources, 2011) is a valuable resource for learning more about Three-Thirds Discipleship.

Who is Francois?

Francois Carr, BTH, MCC, D. Min, NDPB, is the Executive Director of Heart Cry in South Africa. He studied Personnel Management in Cape Town and followed a career as Personnel Officer in the South African Defense Force. During this time, he became involved in a youth ministry that prayed for revival in South Africa. He felt the call of the Lord into a revival-related ministry during a youth conference in November 1992. He became the National Coordinator of Revival South Africa, promoting the message of revival whilst serving full-time as Lieutenant Colonel in the South African Defense Force. He studied part-time, obtaining the following degrees: Bachelor in Theology, Masters in Christian Counseling, and his Doctorate in Ministry.

As the Revival South Africa National Coordinator, he planned and organized revival conferences throughout South Africa until he felt led by the Lord to resign from his position in the Defense Force and enter into full-time ministry. He stepped out in faith and became the Executive Director of Revival SA in June 1999. He founded two ministries called Heart Cry and The Connected Life, which focus on helping people to experience more intimacy with God and mentoring spiritual leaders and churches to become a catalyst for revival. Heart Cry co-sponsors conferences in the USA, Europe and Africa.

Francois is well known for his burden to achieve intimacy with God and revival, and is a popular speaker in Africa, North America and the United Kingdom. He authored several books and articles on prayer, holiness and revival.

He is married to Dorothea and has one daughter, Leoné, who is married to Werner Mostert. Francois currently resides in Pretoria, South Africa.

Contact details
PO Box 90262, Garsfontein, Pretoria, 0042, SA
Websites: www.heartcrysa.com; www.connectedlifeministries.com
Email: office@heartcrysa.co.za

Connected—The Jesus Way

LIFE—DISCIPLE—LEADER
Connected is a 'discipleship-based process' designed to equip and empower believers and churches to become, develop, and replicate effective followers of Christ. They also become workers and leaders of influence who in turn transform their environment. The goal is to encourage and establish a new lifestyle of intimacy with God. It calls all like-minded people to become part of a movement of believers who rediscover how being Connected can transform their church, community, culture, and country!

OUR PURPOSE
God has called us to lead all people to a greater understanding of what it means to enjoy the reality and purpose of as well as intimacy with God.

JESUS' MODEL
The life and ministry of Jesus impacted the people closest to Him, and reached the ends of the earth. His influence grew and stretched beyond Israel to other parts of the world, and still has an impact on people today. We believe we will be most effective by studying and following His methods, strategy, and model.

BE CONNECTED
This journey will take you to a deeper level in your own walk with God. You will rediscover the power and joy of fellowship with God and His people. As you mentor and disciple others to grow to maturity, you will experience the joy of helping believers to encounter God. You will experience greater intimacy and the deeper reality of being Connected with God, as it brings lasting transformation in the lives of ordinary people.

PROCESS
The Connected Process consists of presentations, practical exercises, spiritual coaching, mentoring, follow-up sessions, and self-study. Life

and character transformation takes place as you commit to the process and respond to the Holy Spirit. The journey starts with a Retreat, School of Prayer, or participation in an I Connect Cohort using *The Call* as resource, followed with 9 to 12 weeks of discipleship through coaching and mentoring. The initial retreat is followed with The Connected Disciple (8 sessions)-, and The Connected Leader (9–12 sessions)-, as well as other supplementary materials.

Join a multitude of believers and Subscribe today

USA
Connected Life Ministries, 4000 Parris Bridge Road,
Boiling Springs, S.C. 29316 | www.connectedlifeministries.com
Facebook: Connected Life Ministries

South Africa Heart Cry
www.heartcrysa.com | Facebook: Heart Cry SA |
Facebook: Francois Carr | Email: office@heartcrysa.co.za

www.ingramcontent.com/pod-product-compliance
Lightning Source LLC
LaVergne TN
LVHW051807080426

835511LV00019B/3437